GEORGE W. BUSH
First President of the New Century

GEORGE W. BUSH
First President of the New Century

Tim McNeese

620 South Elm Street, Suite 223
Greensboro, North Carolina 27406
http://www.morganreynolds.com

GEORGE W. BUSH
FIRST PRESIDENT OF THE NEW CENTURY

Copyright © 2002 by Tim McNeese

Library of Congress Cataloging-in-Publication Data

McNeese, Tim.
   George W. Bush : first president of the new century / Tim McNeese.
      p. cm.
   Includes bibliographical references and index.
   Summary: A biography of the former Texas governor who was elected President in the much-contested presidential race in 2000.
   ISBN 1-883846-85-4 (lib. bdg.)
   1. Bush, George W. (George Walker), 1946---Juvenile literature. 2. Presidents--United States--Biography--Juvenile literature. [1. Bush, George W. (George Walker), 1946- 2. Presidents.] I. Title.

E903 .M39 2001
973.931'092--dc21
[B]

                                                              2001040202

Printed in the United States of America
First Edition

*To James Gerhardt,
my sweater-wearing YC
colleague and best
friend from San Antonio,
and to Michael Whitley,
my former colleague and
boot-wearing, New Deal
Democrat denizen of West Texas,
who, by his nature,
helped me understand GWB.*

Contents

George W. Bush was inaugurated as the 43rd president of the United States on Saturday, Janurary 20, 2001. *(AP Photo/Doug Mills)*

Chapter One

East Meets West

"Hanging chads," "dimpled chads," "pregnant chads"—terms used to describe the condition of the waste paper partially removed from punched ballot cards in the state of Florida—helped to define the most extraordinary national election in American history. The 2000 presidential election was the closest race ever. The two leading candidates—Democratic Vice President Al Gore of Tennessee and Republican Governor George W. Bush of Texas—waited five weeks to learn who had won control of the most powerful office in the land.

On election night, November 7, all eyes turned toward Florida, where the state's twenty-five electoral votes held the key to the election. By the next day it was clear that deciding who had won the state's votes would not be easy.

Voter inconsistencies in ballot counting (including disputes about the legality of some ballots cast overseas) became the focal point of the heated post-election process. Some voters claimed to have been confused by a ballot used in Palm Beach County, claiming they mistakenly had voted for the Reform Party candidate, Pat Buchanan, instead of Al Gore. In West Palm Beach, Florida, the state election board disqualified 19,000 votes due to problems with the "butterfly" ballot, so-called because the ballot card folded in half like a butterfly's wings. Neutral observers agreed these were mostly Gore votes. Other county election officials across the state were left with the awkward task of trying to determine the intention of voters whose ballots were not completed properly. These ballots required the use of a stylus to punch out a small rectangle indicating each voter's preference on the ballot. But on many ballots, the rectangle—called a chad—was not completely punched, resulting in what was called a dimpled or pregnant chad. Some chads were still attached by a corner—a dangling chad. How should such votes be counted? Should such votes be counted? The next five weeks turned into a swirl of legal disputes, court hearings, and press conferences.

Ultimately, the United States Supreme Court determined that George W. Bush had won the majority of the state's popular vote, thus earning him the state's electoral votes needed to win the national election. George Walker Bush was sworn into office on Decemebr 13, 2000, as the 43rd president of the United States. Although Vice President Gore had received nearly 500,000 more popular votes than Bush nationwide, for the first time since the 1888 victory of President Benjamin Harrison, the candidate losing the popular vote still became president. In addition, the election of George W. Bush marked the second time in American history that the people had elected the son of a former U.S. president to the White House. George W.'s father, George Herbert Walker Bush, served a single term as president in 1988. In the nineteenth century, John Quincy Adams followed in his father's footsteps when he became president in 1824. John Adams had been elected in 1796.

Although he hails from Texas, George Walker Bush was born into a well-established Connecticut family. He was the first child of George and Barbara Bush and the first grandchild of Prescott and Dorothy Bush. Prescott, a partner in one of Wall Street's most influential investment banks, would be elected to the U.S. Senate in 1952, where he would represent the state of Connecticut for ten years.

George W.'s parents met in 1941 at a country club gathering in Greenwich, Connecticut. Sixteen-year-old Barbara Pierce was home from private boarding school for Christmas. George Bush, who had already enlisted in the navy and would soon become the navy's youngest pilot, was charmed by the outgoing, red-haired Barbara. Despite George's poor dancing skills, Barbara was equally smitten. Three weeks earlier, the Japanese had attacked

Pearl Harbor, Hawaii, and the U.S. had entered World War II.

Two years later, during Christmas of 1943, George Bush and Barbara Pierce were engaged. The navy stationed George in the Pacific, and the couple exchanged letters. Then, in September 1944, Japanese antiaircraft guns shot Bush down while he flew a mission over the Bonin Islands southeast of Japan. He was rescued by a U.S. Navy submarine and later rewarded with a medal. George remained on active duty, and although he and Barbara had planned to marry on December 17, Bush's tour in the Pacific was extended. When he did return for a holiday reunion with his bride-to-be, they were married in Rye, New York, at the First Presbyterian Church. George wore his dress blue uniform. After a night in New York City, the newlyweds took a train to the Georgia coast.

George spent the remainder of the war stateside, although he was assigned to a torpedo bomber unit selected to participate in a planned invasion of Japan that never occurred. After the Japanese surrendered in August of 1945, George Bush left active military service. Like thousands of American military personnel, he was ready for college. George chose an Ivy League school close to home, Yale University in New Haven, Connecticut. He entered school in September 1945.

The Bush newlyweds were not the only war couple at Yale. That year, more than half of Yale's freshman class

George W. Bush was born on July 6, 1946, in New Haven, Connecticut. *(Courtesy of the George Bush Presidential Library.)*

consisted of World War II veterans. Many of them benefited from the newly-created GI Bill that provided government assistance to pay for college tuition. As George Bush was settling into his studies, Barbara learned she was pregnant with her first child. The baby boy arrived on July 6, 1946. The young parents brought George Walker home to their student apartment, one of thirteen that had been carved out of the rambling house located next door to the university's president. Their space was limited, and George found studying at home a challenge. Because the war had delayed his education, George dreamed about his future while busily making a name for himself at Yale, even winning an award for "all around student leadership." As he finished his studies in 1948, most of his teachers and friends thought he would become an investment banker. George, however, had different plans in mind.

He considered farming, but abandoned the risky idea, deciding instead to move to Texas and seek his fortune in the oil business. Texas oil was a rough-and-tumble venture filled with speculation, broken dreams, and sudden fortunes. Although he had different plans for his son's future, Prescott Bush acted supportive. He helped George find a job in Odessa, Texas, as an equipment clerk with International Derrick and Equipment Company, a subsidiary of Dresser Industries. (Prescott sat on the company's board of directors.) When the family packed up their belongings, George W. was two years old. Bar-

In 1950 the Bush family moved to Midland, Texas, where George Bush became involved in the oil industry. Pictured from left to right are Barbara Bush, George W. Bush, George Bush, Grandmother Dorothy Walker Bush, and Grandfather Prescott Bush. *(Courtesy of the George Bush Presidential Library.)*

bara did not look forward to making the trip or to taking up residence in the dry backcountry of West Texas.

George was soon working as a field representative for Dresser Industries, which put him in the oil fields each day. Odessa was a town filled with oilmen and their families. George worked long days, learning all he could about the oil business, and earning a monthly salary of $375. In 1949, the family was transferred to California, where George traveled long-distances to sell drill bits for oilrigs. By 1950, the oil business had transferred the Bush family back to Texas. They moved to Midland, twenty miles north of Odessa, where they lived in a white-collar community. Midland was a boomtown filled with movers and shakers, and George Bush made several contacts that helped him work his way up in the industry.

When the Bush family moved to Midland, they first lived in a motel, but soon they purchased their first house. The small house looked identical in structure to the others along its street, but it was painted light blue. By this time, George W. was no longer the only child—Barbara Bush gave birth to Pauline Robinson Bush in December 1949. The family was close-knit. Barbara stayed at home to watch the children while George prospered in the oil business. Their life consisted of backyard barbecues, parties with neighbors, and kids playing in the neighborhood. Young George W., called "Georgie" by his mother and father, attended the First Presbyterian Church, where his parents each taught a Sunday school class. Over the years, it would be one of several Protestant denominations the Bushes followed. As George W. grew, his days were filled with school, ballgames, family, and friends. He developed a strong affection for his mother, who was always available to him.

The Bush family came to love their days in Midland. Other transfers from back East—many graduates from Ivy League schools such as Yale and Harvard—had also come looking for oil riches. These new Midland residents began transforming their newly adopted prairie town into a blended community of elite Easterners and

"Georgie," as he was called by his parents, grew up in a lively environment surrounded by many children. *(Courtesy of the George Bush Presidential Library.)*

well-established Texans. The melding created a community based on oil speculation, suburban life, and close-knit families. Kids played in vacant lots, raced electric trains at the local YMCA, and roamed in and out of one another's homes. Children enjoyed free reign of Midland's streets, racing their bicycles in every direction; no one worried about crime, and the local movie houses showed Saturday matinees of westerns, comedies, and adventure films. One of the favorite neighborhood moms was Barbara Bush. She could be found at kids' baseball games, keeping score. Children flocked to her, finding her easy to talk to—an adult who would listen to their innocent questions and personal problems.

George W. and his young friends got into the usual mischief, sneaking into the local high school stadium, where the Midland Bulldogs played Friday night football, and swinging from the stadium cross bars and climbing up the light poles. He once broke a neighbor's window with a well-hit baseball. Neighbors remember him as the energetic kid they called "Bushtail." During ball games, young George W. always wanted to be his team's captain, dreaming of becoming the next Willie Mays. He loved attending Camp Longhorn on Inks Lake near Austin, Texas, where he went every summer once he turned seven, as did his siblings. At camp, George W. played for weeks, learned to swim, and created some of his strongest childhood memories.

The early 1950s proved to be exciting years for the

Bush family. George was beginning to make a great deal of money. Late in 1950, he left his job with Dresser Industries and went into the oil business with a friend and neighbor. With financial help from Prescott Bush, George used $350,000 to form the Bush-Overby Oil Development Company, Inc. They had some successes and some failures drilling for oil. Then in 1953, the company merged with other investors into a new firm called Zapata Petroleum Corporation. (The company was named for a movie, a Marlon Brando film titled *Viva, Zapata!* which was playing at the time at a local Midland Theater.)

The Bush family witnessed other important milestones during 1953, including the birth of the third Bush child, John Ellis, who would grow up with the name "Jeb." As the family began to dote on the baby, it became obvious that George W.'s younger sister, Robin, was not well. Within weeks of Jeb's arrival, Robin became sick, tired, and listless. When her concerned parents took her to the doctor, the diagnosis was devastating: Three-year-old Robin had leukemia, a fatal disease. The doctor did not give the young girl more than a month to live.

Still, George and Barbara clung to hope. They took Robin to doctors and specialists, eventually having her treated at a New York clinic. Throughout the entire ordeal, the Bushes never told Robin she might die, nor did they tell George W. These were difficult months for the seven-year-old boy. He rarely saw his mother for weeks at a time. Barbara was strained by the ordeal of caring for a newborn while tending to her dying daughter. When Robin was home, Barbara scolded George W. when he wanted Robin to play anything too physical, or she spent all her time holding her. The Bush family hired a house-keeper to take care of the home, as well as the two boys.

Despite the original doctor's prognosis that Robin would die within three weeks of her diagnosis, she lived for an additional six months. It was not until October 11, 1953 that Robin Bush died in the New York clinic.

When George W.'s parents returned grief-stricken from New York, their oldest son was at school, having started his second grade year. His parents came to the school to pick him up that day and told him that Robin had died. George W. felt both crushed and curious. He wanted to know how long his parents had known about the leuke-mia and why they had kept it from him.

The Bush family was sorrowful and drained. They had received significant support from family members and friends in Midland, but the loss was almost too much to bear. Still, they kept going, refusing to show emotion in public, saving their crying for private moments. Even-tually, the family pieced their lives back together. Bar-bara rekindled her relationships with her sons and tried to answer their questions about the loss of their sister. George W. asked his mother which way Robin had been buried, standing up or lying down? Once at a football game, George W. said that he wished he were his sister.

When his father asked what he meant, he replied: "I bet she can see the game better from up there than we can here."

Despite such innocent observations, George W. noticed that his parents, especially his mother, had changed. There was something missing from her demeanor. He heard her cry from time to time. He became concerned about her, even to the point of refusing to go out and play with his friends, telling them he needed to stay home and be with his mother.

Less than sixteen months after Robin's death, Barbara gave birth to her fourth child, Neil Mallon. Slowly, things returned to normal. At the same time, they were becoming wealthier. Within twelve months of the founding of Zapata Oil, the company drilled seventy-one oil wells, producing 1,250 barrels of oil a day. They had also started a new division, Zapata Off-Shore, to search for oil in the Gulf of Mexico. The profits flowed into the Bush family. Soon they were independently wealthy. This money would soon finance George Bush's move into politics.

In 1955 the family moved into a new 3,000-square-foot brick house, complete with a swimming pool. The next year, Marvin Pierce Bush was born a few days after the third anniversary of Robin's death.

George W. progressed through elementary school. He could be mischievous and made several visits to the principal's office. In third grade, he threw a football

George W. was raised in a wealthy, close-knit family and was especially close to his mother, Barbara. *(Courtesy of the George Bush Presidential Library.)*

through a window at school. In fourth grade, his teacher sent him to the principal for having drawn a mustache, goatee, and long sideburns on his own face with a ballpoint pen. The principal gave him a paddling. He tussled with his younger brother at home, even though George W. was seven years older.

George W. tried to keep up with his schoolwork at Sam Houston Elementary School, but he was easily distracted. He learned first of Texas history through a year-long study in third grade. Teachers considered him a pleasant boy, scrappy and aggressive on the baseball diamond, but with a smart mouth. He was not an avid reader, preferring sports over books.

More than anything else, George W. loved baseball. His father had played at Yale, where his mother kept score at her husband's games. As George W. grew, Barbara continued to keep score for her son's games. He played the game with enthusiasm. Throughout his years in little league, George W. played catcher, which required him to be aggressive. His father, when available, helped him hone his skills in practice at home by playing catch in the backyard. George Bush also encouraged his son's love of baseball statistics and would quiz George W. on player records and trivia.

George W. and his friends collected discarded soda bottles and redeemed them for money to purchase baseball cards. He even thought of a way to collect cards with players' autographs. He glued the cards to postcards and mailed them to his favorite players, asking them to sign his cards and return them. George W.'s favorite professional baseball team was the New York Giants. More than thirty years later, he could still recite the names of the 1954 Giants starting lineup.

George W. was growing up in a world of wealth, power, industry, hard work, and strong family commitments. He watched as his father, the same man who would play catch in the backyard, became an important businessman in Texas. As early as 1956, the Junior Chamber of Commerce named George Bush to be one of the "Five Outstanding Young Men of Texas." Although his Eastern roots had helped George Bush to launch his career, George W. has always asserted that his father achieved success through hard work and determination, more than the use of his family name.

Because of his success, George Bush was often away from home. By 1958, the town of Midland had nearly doubled in population, boasting 40,000 new citizens. The phone book listed 750 oil companies, and Bush was one of the most well-known oilmen in the city. He had become a man of regional importance and power. His father was a U.S. Senator. Then, in 1959, George Bush accepted a job in Houston, Texas, and the family was on the move again.

Chapter Two

"The Lip"

In Houston, the Bush family found themselves living in the city that boasted the center of power and influence in the state of Texas. The largest city in the state with almost one million residents, Houston was also at the center of conservative politics. George Bush was beginning the pursuit of a new dream. He wanted to follow his father into a career as a Republican politician. Houston would be more hospitable to these plans than would heavily Democratic West Texas. As the family prepared for the move, a final addition came into the family. Dorothy Ellis Bush, George and Barbara's one surviving daughter, was born in August 1959.

The family moved into a new house on a large lot on Briar Drive. George W. entered the eighth grade at Kinkaid School, a top private school in Houston. One of the oldest private schools in the state of Texas, Kinkaid was founded by Margaret Hunter Kinkaid, the daughter of a

Confederate soldier and gold prospector. Thirteen-year-old George W. took to Kinkaid quickly. He made friends and became well known as an athlete. He was elected as a class officer. But even George W. was stunned at how wealthy his classmates were and how quick they were to show off their money. Although his own family was wealthy, the Bushes considered displays of wealth inappropriate. They were a levelheaded and practical clan.

During George W.'s first two years at Kinkaid, his father's work and budding political career caused him to be frequently absent from the family. His trips sometimes took him around the world. Meanwhile, Barbara remained at home with five children, a responsibility she always considered important and essential, but one that she was beginning to resent. She would later write about her frustrations:

> This was a period, for me, of long days and short years; of diapers, runny noses, earaches, more Little League games than you could believe possible . . . Sunday school and church, of hours of urging homework . . . of feeling that I'd never, ever be able to have fun again; and coping with the feeling that George Bush, in his excitement of starting a small company and traveling around the world, was having a lot of fun.

With his father increasingly absent from home, George

W., the oldest of the Bush children, began to feel responsible for his family's well-being. When his mother experienced a miscarriage, George W. drove her to the hospital and later questioned her about the wisdom of having any more children.

But George W. was soon to leave the Bush home in Texas for a cooler, northern climate. After attending Kinkaid for two years, he transferred to Phillips Academy in Andover, Massachusetts. What Kinkaid represented to the elite and powerful of Texas, Phillips Academy, also known as Andover, represented for the wealthy and influential of the Northeast. The school's history extended back to the 1700s, when George Washington sent his grandnephews there to be educated.

Andover was a Bush family tradition. George Bush had been captain of several varsity teams in the 1930s and 1940s and president of his senior class. George W.'s uncle had attended Andover, and his cousin was entering his junior year when George W. enrolled. While he did not want to leave Houston, it was his father's wish that he follow in his footsteps. In addition, attending Andover almost assured young men they would be accepted to either Yale or Harvard.

When the fifteen-year-old arrived at the campus in the fall of 1961, his father introduced him to some of the same teachers he had studied under a generation before. His mother told him she would miss her oldest son, and he told her he would feel the same.

At Andover, George W. was a fish out of water. The few Texans there lived in the same dormitory, America House, where Dr. Samuel Francis Smith had written the patriotic song, "My Country 'Tis of Thee," in 1832.

Young George W. soon discovered that he was not prepared for the academic challenge of Andover. He thought his skill on the baseball diamond would guarantee his success, but Andover put academics first. Students were required to wear a coat and tie to classes and attend morning chapel. Dorm lights went off at ten p.m., and radios and televisions were not allowed. In some dorms, the radiators were turned off at night. One could receive demerits for a long list of infractions.

George W. buckled down and tried to approach his studies seriously. He did well in history, performed adequately in math, and struggled in English. His English instructor flunked George's first essay, its subject being the death of his sister Robin and its impact on his mother. The instructor called George's essay "disgraceful." He lived with the constant dread of flunking out of Andover and bringing shame to his parents. He did make friends and gain acceptance by others who saw him as an athlete and an amiable young man.

By his junior year, George W. was popular at Andover and was considered a natural leader. He lettered in baseball and played junior varsity basketball and football. His small size kept him from playing varsity football, so he became one of the cheerleaders, a megaphone-toting squad of eight young men who rallied the fans during games. His cheerleading duties became important to George W., and it became his most prominent role on campus. Quick to make a joke, even to the detriment of others, George W.'s nickname was "The Lip," because he always had a smart answer and usually had an opinion about everything. Years later, a newly-entering freshman recalled Bush's busy extracurricular life: "I'm sure he took some things seriously, but he was more interested in social standing than what grades he had to get in order to get into Yale." George W. enjoyed parties and dating. At some parties alcohol was served, although it was against Andover's rules.

Unlike other students of the era, Bush did not openly criticize American social structure. During the early 1960s, many students were angered by their parents' resistance to the Civil Rights Movement and the developing war in Southeast Asia. One student expressed this sentiment in an article from 1962: "Take one good look at the world and you'll see there's no interest in decency, only in power and in pushing the other guy around." Bush was never won over by those who were critical of his father's values, achievements, wealth, and ambitions.

By his senior year most students at Andover did not make a practice of getting excited at the school's sporting events, and many did not even attend. George W. was determined to change that. The cheerleaders began holding daily pep rallies, performing skits at Chapel, and

cajoling the students into giving their enthusiastic support to the various Andover teams. His efforts paid off,
and soon most of the senior class began attending ball
games. Anyone who was not present was booed when
they entered the commons for lunch.

His efforts did not go unnoticed by the administrators
and faculty at Andover. While some faculty complained
that the cheerleading squad was holding too many pep
rallies, the school's president, Dan Cooper, approached
Bush about the school's drinking problem. Andover's
rules did not allow campus drinking, but the graduating
Class of 1964 was infamous for alcohol consumption.
Cooper offered students an opportunity to get rid of their
alcohol before a scheduled search of all dorm rooms.
Bush's role was to rally students into pouring out their
booze. He accepted the challenge. It was a success. Prior
to the alcohol amnesty plan, almost one out of every ten
Andover seniors were on the verge of being expelled for
alcohol infractions. George W.'s class graduated with the
fewest alcohol-related expulsions in Andover's history.
This success did not mean that he stopped drinking,
however.

Approaching graduation, George W. assumed that he
would soon be attending Yale. Although some teachers at
Andover were skeptical that such a mediocre student
could find his way into the Ivy League institution, George
W. felt confident. His grandfather was on the Yale Board
of Trustees, and his father was one of its best-remem-

bered students. George W. learned of his acceptance after spring break. Among his classmates in the Class of '64, thirty were accepted into Yale, forty-nine went on to Harvard, twenty to Princeton, and a handful of others attended various Ivy League schools such as Columbia, Pennsylvania State, Brown, and Dartmouth.

The early 1960s brought more changes to the Bush family. In 1962, Grandfather Prescott Bush had decided to step down from the senate and not run for a third term, citing his desire to play golf and go sailing with his wife, Dottie. The same year, George Bush decided to enter Texas politics by running for the chairmanship of the Harris County Republican Party. As soon as he won that position he began planning to run for a U.S. Senate seat in 1964. The year George W. graduated from Andover, his father was busy campaigning. While spending the summer in Houston before entering Yale, George W. had his first taste of elective politics.

Chapter Three

The "Nomadic Period"

The Bush campaign for the U.S. Senate seat from Texas kicked off in the summer of 1964 with a bus tour called "The Bandwagon for Bush," just after George W.'s eighteenth birthday. The bus crisscrossed the state, stopping at forty cities from Houston to Abilene. George Bush faced an uphill climb as many of the stops on the bus tour were in traditional Democratic strongholds.

After spending the majority of three years back east, the campaign was an opportunity for George W. to make connections once again with the state he considered to be home. He traveled through all of Texas during the summer of 1964. The Bush campaign, attempting to create a traveling road show atmosphere, also included entertainers, such as a country and western band called the Black Mountain Boys and the Bush Bluebonnet Belles dance group.

In August, George W. left the campaign and headed

for the city of his birth to enter Yale University. As he had at Andover, he entered a new school in the shadow of his father, who had played varsity soccer as well as baseball and had been invited into a secret society known as the Skull & Bones Society, as Prescott Bush had before him.

At Yale, George W. continued to be an average student, more interested in sports and socializing than in his studies. But he did have a charming personality and was well-known and liked for his quick wit. For example, when he pledged membership in the campus fraternity Delta Kappa Epsilon (his father's fraternity), he memorized the names of all fifty of his fellow pledges, reciting them on command. No other pledge could remember more than a half dozen names.

Once on campus, George W. reconnected with old friends from Andover and made new friends, too. The rules of Andover were now a thing of the past, and George W. attended parties where alcohol was served without restriction. The Delta Kappa Epsilon fraternity was known for its athletes and campus rowdies. They also had a reputation as the heaviest drinkers, and their fraternity house bar remained open twenty-four hours a day.

Late in his first semester, George went home to Texas to be with his family on election night. His father's Senate race had been periodically reported in the Yale student newspaper. That year, eight Yale graduates were campaigning for high office. The various dormitories on campus held their own mock elections. In voting between the elder Bush and his opponent, Democrat Ralph Yarborough, Bush won by ninety-one votes out of 2,300 cast. Back in Texas, however, the real race had different results. George Bush had to campaign against the image of being an outsider to Texas, a wealthy investment banker's son from Connecticut, despite the fact he had called Texas home for nearly a generation. His opponent called him a "carpetbagger from Connecticut who is drilling oil for the Sheik of Kuwait." Bush received solid support from his fellow Republicans and a new support group called "Democrats for Bush." Former Vice President Richard Nixon and Republican presidential candidate Barry Goldwater had both come to Texas to rally for him. But, by late evening on election day, it was obvious that Bush had lost.

After the election, George W. returned to Yale, disappointed with the vote, but proud of his father. He had watched his father take personal hits during the campaign. Back on the campus, however, he was hurt more by a comment made by a member of the faculty than he had been by all the attacks in Texas. George W. remembered that Yale's chaplain, Reverend William Sloane Coffin, who had attended Yale with George Bush, stopped him on the sidewalk to say: "I knew your father, and your father lost to a better man."

Despite the setback, George Bush was determined to be elected to political office. In the meantime, George W.

During his first year at Yale University, George W. played on the freshman baseball team.
(Courtesy of the George Bush Presidential Library.)

returned to his studies, including classes in philosophy, Spanish, and English. His second semester course, Political Science 13B, focused on the threat of communism and how post-World War II diplomacy had attempted to contend with it.

At the end of his first year at Yale, George W. returned to Texas for the summer and was dispatched by his father to work on an inland oil barge in Louisiana. George W. did not like the work and looked forward to his weeklong breaks between stints in Houston, where he played tennis and visited with his friends. The job was supposed to last from June through August, but he left a week early. When Bush heard that his son left early, he summoned George W. to his office to express his disappointment. Then, two hours later, they went to a Houston Astros game together. Yet George W. never forgot the encounter, later recalling his father's lecture as "the sternest words to me, even though he said them in a very calm way."

Despite his lackluster freshman grades, George W. Bush returned to Yale in the fall of 1965 and the Delta Kappa Epsilon house. He spent much of his time playing card games, drinking, talking about sports with his friends, and dating girls. Academics continued to take a backseat. He did not even join the campus Young Republicans.

Back home in Houston at Christmas break, he began seriously dating a young woman named Cathryn Wolfman, whose family lived in the same Houston neighborhood. Cathryn was a vibrant young woman who attended Rice University. She shared his love of sports and had a wide circle of friends.

The summer following George W.'s sophomore year, he worked as a sporting goods salesman at a Sears store while his father planned his run for the United States House of Representatives. As a Houston resident, Bush would represent citizens similar to himself: mostly white, affluent, and somehow connected to the oil business. As he had in his Senate campaign, George Bush made a determined run for the Texas 7th District seat. He campaigned restlessly, and George W. often stood by him as his number one supporter. This time, in November 1966, his dad would win the election.

As a junior at Yale, George W. served as the president of his fraternity, proof of his popularity among his friends and an early indication of his leadership skills. He settled on history as his major, and his courses included anthropology, twentieth-century American culture, nineteenth-century European diplomacy, a course in city planning, and twentieth-century American literature.

As the year progressed, fraternities became less influential on university campuses across the U.S. At Yale, fraternities, such as Delta Kappa Epsilon, that engaged in heavy drinking, carousing, and other antics began to receive deeper scrutiny by the administration. Also, incoming freshmen became less interested in fraternity life. As the war in Vietnam accelerated, and the protest against the war became more popular, being part of a social fraternity seemed less important to many as world events took on relevance. George W. continued to have a strong sense of pride for his fraternity despite the recent change in attitudes.

George Herbert Walker Bush celebrated his election to the U.S. House of Representatives in November 1966, with his son at his side. Returning to Yale after a week at home was difficult for the younger Bush. He was fully convinced that he belonged in Texas. He disagreed with what he saw as the predominant "liberal" culture of the Northeast, and he disliked the intellectual Ivy League environment. He was also becoming more deeply attached to Cathryn Wolfman. He told some of his closest friends that "there was something out of sync at Yale and in the Northeast."

In January of George W.'s junior year, he and Cathryn announced their engagement to be married that summer. They made plans to live in New Haven during George's senior year. By summer however, the marriage was postponed until after their senior years because Cathryn wanted to finish her education at Rice. After a third postponement, the couple cancelled the wedding altogether. In later interviews, Cathryn would explain it simply: "I loved him . . . I was glad I was engaged to him. The relationship died and that was that." Although marriage might have slowed George W.'s social life, for the time being it was not to be. He continued devoting much of his energy to socializing with friends.

During his final semester at Yale, George W. was invited to join one of the school's highly secret societies. Seven such societies existed at Yale, but Skull & Bones was the most exclusive, dating back to 1832. Its members typically included the Yale men from families of the greatest wealth and power: The movers and shakers of America's business world and politics. Past initiates included former President William Howard Taft, William F. Buckley Jr., Dean Witter Jr., and various presidential cabinet members. The rituals of membership remained secret, but being selected as a Bonesman provided a member with a lifetime of contacts and support. Most importantly to George W., his father and grandfather were both Bonesmen.

As George W. approached graduation with a history degree in 1968, he remained unsure of his future plans. He did not want to work in New York or Washington, his plans for marriage were off, and there was the constant, overwhelming concern that he would be drafted to serve in the military in the ever-expanding Vietnam War. There were now more than half a million American troops in Southeast Asia. Upon graduation George W. would lose his student deferment and going to Vietnam would become a real possibility—and a source of great anxiety. He may have followed in his father's footsteps in other ways (attending Andover and Yale), but he did not want to join the military and participate in an unpopular war.

As did many other young men of his generation,

including future president Bill Clinton and future vice president Dan Quayle, George W. wanted to find a way to avoid the draft. One way to do this was by joining a National Guard unit. This way he could train as a soldier, but he would be able to avoid going to Vietnam. The problem was that only a limited number of openings were available in the Texas National Guard.

Nevertheless, twelve days before his graduation, George W. was inducted into the Texas Air National Guard. The Yale graduate did poorly on his qualification tests. He barely passed his Air Force officers qualification test answering only twenty-five percent of the questions correctly. He received a fifty percent score on his navigator aptitude test. On his "officer quality" test, however, he achieved a score of ninety-five percent. Although claims were later made that Bush was accepted into the Texas Air Guard as a favor to his congressman father, he has always denied this was true. Another new member of the so-called "Champagne" Unit of the Texas Air National Guard was the son of Lloyd Bentsen, a wealthy businessman and future U.S. Senator.

George W. left for Moody Air Force Base in Valdosta, Georgia, in November 1968, to begin the year-long training program. In December 1969, he earned his National Guard wings and returned to Houston, where he served on weekends. Although the National Guard duty kept him from Vietnam, it did postpone his career decisions until at least 1970.

George W. graduated from Yale in 1968 with a degree in history.
(Courtesy of the George Bush Presidential Library.)

Growing tensions surrounding the conflict in Vietnam led to riots in several American cities, such as this demonstration in Chicago in 1968. *(Courtesy of the Library of Congress.)*

The late 1960s were turbulent times. The Vietnam War was unpopular among an increasing number of Americans. In 1968, the year Bush graduated, civil rights leader Martin Luther King, Jr. was assassinated in Memphis. Two months later, Robert Kennedy, younger brother to former president John Kennedy and a candidate for president, was killed in Los Angeles. Several cities suffered through riots, war protests, and student strikes. Young men grew their hair long and young people experimented with drugs. These were confusing times for George W. Bush, a young man who graduated from one of the nation's most elite schools, put on the uniform of the Texas National Guard, and embraced the status quo. He continued to be out of step with the anti-establishment attitudes of America's young people.

He had followed the lead of his father and grandfather, attended their schools, joined their secret society, and identified with their politics, but he felt disconnected with most of his own generation. George W. turned twenty-four in 1970 and would spend the next few years vaguely pursuing undefined ambitions. They were years of discontent, of personal floundering, that both he and his father have referred to as his "nomadic period."

Chapter Four

Emerging from the Shadow

Back in Houston in early 1970, George W. began combat crew training in the Air National Guard at Ellington Air Force Base. He rented an apartment with a fellow Guardsman and completed the flight program in June of that year.

George W. Bush spent his years in the Texas Air National Guard flying fighter jets, including F-102s, often referred to as "The Deuce." He also expended much of his time drinking and partying. In later years, George admitted these were years of working hard and playing hard. Through his Air Guard years, Bush continued to suffer from a lack of focus. Most of his fellow pilots knew George was the son of a U.S. Congressman, but no one seemed to think much about it. One of his colleagues said, "He was certainly competent. He didn't put on airs." George W. remained on active duty for two years. His service record includes positive statements

As a pilot in the Texas Air National Guard, George W. flew fighter jets during his two years of active duty. *(Courtesy of the George Bush Presidential Library.)*

from his commanders. One noted, "George W. clearly stands out as a top-notch fighter interceptor pilot . . . Lt. Bush's skills far exceed his contemporaries . . . He is a natural leader whom his contemporaries look to for leadership."

As the young Bush lived the life of a Texas Air National Guard pilot, the elder Bush's political career changed directions. In 1970, he ran for the U.S. Senate against Lloyd Bentsen, the father of George W.'s air guard comrade, but he was defeated. This loss ended his career in the House of Representatives, to which he had been reelected in 1968. President Nixon, who had urged

him to run against Bentsen, rewarded Bush with important political positions over the next few years. Bush
served as the U.S. ambassador to the United Nations in
1971, as chairman of the Republican National Commit-
tee in 1973, and as liaison office chief (essentially the
acting U.S. ambassador) in the People's Republic of
China. Following the resignation of Richard Nixon during the Watergate scandal in 1974, new President Gerald
Ford appointed Bush to head the Central Intelligence
Agency. These were all important and prestigious jobs,
but they did little to satisfy his desire for high level
elective office. His connection to Richard Nixon actually hurt him politically after Watergate, when Republicans were linked to the scandal. One effect of his asso-
ciation with the White House did have a more positive
impact on George Bush. He developed a new political
goal for himself: He decided he wanted to become president of the United States.

George W. took a job in 1971 working for Stratford of
Texas, a giant agribusiness company. He piloted company planes across the United States and to company
holdings in South America, Central America, and the
Caribbean. His boss was Robert Gow, who had worked
for his father at Zapata Oil. He remained with the company only nine months. One weekend every month,
Bush flew for the Texas Air National Guard.

During 1972, George W. considered running for the
Texas state legislature, but instead worked in Alabama

President Richard Nixon helped George Bush to obtain important roles in the federal government until he resigned from office following the Watergate scandal. *(Courtesy of the Library of Congress.)*

on the losing Senate campaign of a family friend, Winton "Red" Blount. Disappointed, he went to spend Christmas with his family in Washington, D.C, where they had moved. During this family gathering George's drinking provoked a confrontation with his father. One night George W. took his sixteen-year-old brother Marvin out for an evening of bar-hopping. They drove home drunk and, as they neared home, George W. hit a neighbor's metal trash can and continued to push the container screeching down the street and into his father's driveway. His father was furious and called his son into the family den. A drunken George W. entered the room saying, "I hear you're looking for me. You wanna go *mano a mano* [Spanish for "hand to hand"] right here." The two men shouted at one another until Barbara broke them up, sending them to opposite corners of the room. For the rest of the holiday vacation, the Bush household remained tense. Later in life, George W. reflected upon this encounter and this phase of his youth: "[I was trying to] reconcile who I was and who my dad was, to establish my own identity in my own way."

After considering a law degree, George W. decided to apply to graduate studies at Harvard School of Business and was accepted for the 1973 fall term. In the months before leaving for Harvard, he worked as a youth counselor for the Professionals United for Leadership League, or "Project PULL," an inner-city-project of his father's. For several months, Bush concentrated on working with

The Bush boys and their father in 1970. Pictured from left to right are Neil, George Bush, Jeb, George W., and Marvin. *(Courtesy of the George Bush Presidential Library.)*

poor youths. He played basketball, taught wrestling, and took participants on field trips. He even made an attempt to stop drinking. He favorably impressed the full-timers at PULL. One co-worker later noted: "[He] was so down-to-earth, to be honest, I just thought he was a poor kid trying to make his way in the world."

George W. enjoyed working with disadvantaged youth and felt he was making a difference in their lives. A friend, Charlie Younger, said of Bush: "He would love to see some underdog with the right cause overcome some giant with maybe not quite the right message. If someone was bashing a minority, he would demand: 'Why do you think that way?' All people have worth to George."

Upon entering Harvard Business School, George W. faced an extraordinary challenge. In some ways, life at Harvard resembled life at Yale. Just as he had been at Yale, George W. was popular with the student body. He applied himself to his work at Harvard, however. He prepared extensive weekly assignments and took study groups seriously. Now he was a young man with something to prove: That he could perform independently of his accomplished father.

Something else seemed different about George W. Bush. He was no longer anxious to fit in. He wore cowboy boots and his Texas Air National Guard bomber jacket to his classes, chewed tobacco (he even carried a spit cup around campus), and listened to country music. His roots did not embarrass him. He knew he was from Texas, and it did not matter to him who might think less of him for it. He was no longer secretive about his conservative politics. George W. was becoming his own man. His mother noticed the changes in her son, and she was happy to see them. One thing that did not change, however, was his drinking habit. Hard drinking fit in well with his image.

George W. finished his Masters in Business Administration degree in 1975. For the first time since his graduation from Yale seven years earlier, he had a clear plan. He wanted to follow in his father's footsteps and return to Midland, Texas, and make his fortune in the oil business.

It seemed to be a good time to enter the oil business in West Texas. The days of wildcatting in the scrub plains were gone, but the United States was now consuming more oil than it produced. About half of America's oil was imported from OPEC (Organization of Petroleum Exporting Countries). In 1973, in response to U.S. support of Israel in the Yom Kippur War, OPEC, which was predominantly Arab, drastically reduced the amount of oil it shipped to the United States. Motorists spent most of 1974 sitting in long gas lines as the price of fuel rose daily. With the renewed interest in finding domestic oil supplies, by 1975, the year George W. returned to Texas, domestic oil production was on the rise. Just as his father had a generation before, George W. Bush arrived in Midland just in time for the new boom.

For one of his first jobs in Midland, George W. worked as a "land man," sorting through court documents to determine who owned the mineral rights to various pieces of property. A single piece of land might have dozens of owners. While one person owned the surface property itself, another could own the mineral rights. One might own the oil found at 2,000 feet, while another could own the oil at 6,000 feet. Once he discovered who owned the mineral rights, George W. negotiated with the owner about leasing those rights. Earning $100 a day, George W. was on his way to becoming an independent businessman. His youthful charm helped him secure agreements, partnerships, and signed contracts.

The two years between 1975 to 1977 altered George W. He was making money—not great money, but good money—in a job he enjoyed. In 1977, he made his first effort at oil field development. He teamed up with two friends, Fletcher Mills and Ralph Way, with plans to drill into the same gigantic oil-rich Permian Basin his father had tapped. The team's first drilling efforts turned out to be failures, and George W. lost his investment capital. But the drilling continued until they discovered oil. George W.'s main contribution to the partnership was his ability to convince investors to put up the monies necessary to do exploratory drilling. More than once, George W.'s easy-going nature convinced money men to invest.

Although these years were formative for George W. in the business world, he remained rough around the edges. He became notorious for wearing worn-out pants, shirts with frayed collars, and socks that did not match. He drove a 1970 Cutlass that looked "like he'd painted it himself." His living quarters, a rundown apartment in a converted garage, usually littered with dirty laundry, old pizza boxes, and trash. He repaired his broken bed with neckties. While Bush had been tamed in his professional life, he was still less than domesticated.

Nineteen hundred seventy-seven would prove to be a watershed year for George W. Bush. He was known and respected in Midland, although his oil ventures had only met with modest success. He had accumulated around $500,000, and had a stake in five gas wells and three oil

George W. talks with a worker at an oil field. *(Courtesy of the George Bush Presidential Library.)*

wells. Friends urged him to enter politics. The Texas 19th Congressional District was going to become vacant after forty-four years of conservative Democratic control. Bush vacillated, then decided to throw his hat in the ring. (He first checked with his father to make certain he did not intend to run for the Texas governorship in 1978. That would have placed one too many Bushes in Texas politics at the same time. His father, however, was planning to run for the presidency of the United States in 1980.) He finally made the decision to run. George W. was following his father and grandfather into elective politics.

Nineteen hundred seventy-seven was an important year for another reason. Although George W. had mostly stopped dating as he focused on his business, his friends occasionally still tried to set him up with women. Then a married couple, Joe and Jan O'Neill (Joe and George W. had played baseball together as kids growing up in Midland), invited him to a barbecue at their house, where they arranged for him to meet thirty-year-old Laura Welch, who lived in Austin.

Laura Welch was born in Midland on November 4, 1946. She was the only child of Harold and Jenna Welch, who had remained in Midland over the years. Her father worked as a successful architect and building contractor. Her mother, Jenna, was a dedicated bird watcher and officer in the Midland Naturalist Society. While Laura and George W. had grown up in the same small town, had attended the same schools, and had served on the same student council, they did not remember meeting before that cookout in 1977.

Upon meeting Laura, George W. was captivated. His own words described his response to the soft-spoken brunette: "If it wasn't love at first sight, it happened shortly thereafter." Laura had attended Southern Methodist University in Dallas. She received a bachelor's degree in education, then stayed to earn a masters in library science. Always an A-student, Laura Welch had known from her childhood that she wanted to be a teacher. When she met George W., she was self-assured, in no rush to get married, and maybe even a little elusive.

According to Barbara Bush, George W. was "struck by lightning." That first night the two stayed out talking until after midnight. They saw each other the next day, playing miniature golf with the O'Neills, and continued to see one another over the next week. Within five weeks they were engaged.

Chapter Five

A Life of His Own

At first, George's friends were surprised at how quickly his relationship with Laura developed. His old friend Charlie Younger explained it this way: "I think the timing was a critical factor, because both of them were at a crossroads in their lives. He was ready to settle down and think about a family and have a decent lady to make a life with. Call it fate, destiny, whatever, but they came along and crossed at the right time."

George Walker Bush and Laura Welch were married at 11 a.m. on November 6, 1977, at the United Methodist Church in Midland. It was a simple ceremony, with seventy-five friends and family members in attendance. They honeymooned in Mexico. When they returned, George's congressional campaign was already under-way. Laura Bush never taught public school or served as a librarian again. She dedicated herself to George and his various careers, especially his political future. Barbara gave her one piece of advice after the wedding: Never criticize your husband's speeches. It was a rule Laura tried to follow although once, during the 1978 campaign, George asked her how that night's speech had gone. When she remarked, "Well, your speech wasn't very good," he drove their car into the garage wall.

George W.'s first foray into Texas politics was an uphill climb. His name provided immediate recognition for many and helped him to raise money. But he remained cautious about linking himself with his father, for fear voters would simply consider him to be a carbon copy. He faced serious opposition in the Republican primary. One rival, James Reese, referred to George as "Junior." George also received a blow when Ronald Reagan, who would run for the U.S. presidency just two years later, endorsed Reese. (Reagan may have been motivated because he knew that he would be running against George W.'s father for the Republican nomination for president in 1980.) But Reese's highly negative, even sarcastic, campaign style did not win over enough voters. Bush won the nomination on June 3, 1978, garnering 6,787 votes to Reese's 5,350.

In the general election, George W. faced a strong Democratic challenger, state senator Kent Hance. Hance's strategy appeared similar to Reese's: Hammer away at George W.'s lack of political experience and play up connections to his father and the family's non-Texan roots. Despite the fact that George W. had actually spent most of his life in Texas, Hance's tactics worked. Hance won the election by nearly 7,000 votes. Although he lost, George took comfort in knowing that his father had lost his first election as well.

George had little time to be gloomy. He formed his own oil company, Arbusto. (*Arbusto* is Spanish for "bush.") The company was not an immediate success. Although he was able to convince investors to put up capital, they drilled several dry wells.

In the meantime, George's father was reentering the political arena. Bush was one of several Republicans who sought to deny front-runner Ronald Reagan the 1980 nomination. Early in the campaign, George Bush attacked Reagan for being too conservative and said he did not have a chance of winning the national election.

After he surprised Reagan and won the Iowa caucus, George Bush was the only candidate with the potential to stop the former California governor. But Reagan, who had attempted to win the nomination twice before, eventually proved to be unbeatable. Bush, however, was the runner-up, and Reagan decided to ask him to be his vice presidential running mate. Bush accepted the offer and became the 1980 Republican vice presidential candidate.

The Reagan-Bush campaign proved to be a juggernaut. President Jimmy Carter was hamstrung by runaway inflation and high interest rates. Finally, when a group of Iranian students, backed by the new Islamic fundamentalist government, seized the American embassy and held almost 200 American citizens hostage for over a

George W. began his own political career in 1978 when he ran for the U.S. Congress.

(Courtesy of the George Bush Presidential Library.)

year, Carter's chances of reelection were doomed. In January 1981, George Herbert Walker Bush became vice president of the United States.

The same year his father took office, George W. and Laura began to plan a family. They had wanted to have children for some time and became concerned when Laura did not conceive. In the meantime, brother Jeb and his wife, Columba, had two children. George W. and Laura could not help but notice how much his parents loved being grandparents. Finally, the Bushes decided to adopt a child. Just weeks before the adoption process was completed, however, Laura announced she was pregnant—with twins. They halted the adoption. On November 25, 1981, a few weeks following George and Laura's fourth anniversary, Laura gave birth to two daughters. The new daughters were named for their grandmothers, Barbara and Jenna. For George W., the birth of his twins was a defining moment in his life. He later wrote:

> Laura and I didn't know anything about babies, and suddenly we had two. In the early days, they cried, and cried, and cried some more. I still shudder today when I remember the helpless feeling that comes to all new parents when your precious little charges wail and cry and you can't seem to do anything to console them . . . I would pace through the house, holding both of them in my arms,

juggling them, making faces, singing the only song I knew that seemed appropriate for children, the Yale fight song: "Bulldog, bulldog. Bow wow wow."

George W. enjoyed being a father. He wrestled with his children on the floor, made faces at them, and tickled them silly. He wrote how "a friend once told me he never realized how to enjoy his children until he watched me play with mine." The Bushes arranged for their girls' baptism in the Methodist church—their mother's church—when they turned nine months old. Prior to the twins' baptism, the Bushes had alternated between Laura's

George W. and Laura Bush with their twin daughers, age eight, in August 1990.
(Courtesy of the George Bush Presidential Library.)

George W. began his own oil business, called Arbusto, which eventually became Bush Exploration. *(Courtesy of the George Bush Presidential Library.)*

Methodist church and George W.'s Presbyterian church.

As his father took office in Washington, D.C., George W. expanded his investments in the oil business. His company continued to drill for oil, sinking almost 100 wells by 1982. Bush grew concerned that Arbusto had gained a reputation for failed drilling as much as it had for successful ventures. People around Midland had started calling it "Are Busted." He opted to change the unfortunate name to Bush Exploration and set out to raise $6 million in investment capital. The dynamics of the business had changed by then, however, and there was a glut of crude oil on the market. Prices dropped so sharply that it was no longer profitable to invest in the more risky companies. George W. was only able to raise $1 million.

Over the next few years the oil business grew worse. A falling out in OPEC made even more oil available, and the price of a barrel of crude oil dropped fifty percent. Such a move knocked the props out from under active oilmen such as George W. Bush.

Yet George W. landed on his feet. Although he had sold his majority interest in Arbusto, he had been retained as the chairman of Bush Exploration, a role that paid him $75,000 annually and gave him 1.1 million shares of stock. Then, as Bush Exploration teetered on the brink of bankruptcy, it was purchased by Harken Oil and Gas, a gigantic Dallas fuel company. George received a nice salary package as part of the exchange. Harken granted him $300,000 in stock, a seat on the company's board of directors, and a consultant fee of $120,000 per year. The deal freed him from the prospect of bankruptcy. It also gave him enough money to make other investments. But he had only avoided bankruptcy by the intervention of a company with ties to his father, who was now vice president of the United States. In 1986, it appeared that, despite George W.'s best efforts, the gap between his father's accomplishments and his own was widening.

Chapter Six

A Clearer, More Meaningful Life

When George W. was a child, his parents had taken him to the Presbyterian church. When George and Barbara visited Connecticut to see their family, they attended the Episcopal church. Neither church had ever touched George W. deeply. Then, in 1985, George began to change his outlook on religion.

Two people influenced this direction toward Christianity. The first was his wife, Laura. Once they married in the First Methodist church, he began attending with her. He became involved in church committees, and, by the early 1980s, he began attending Bible study classes. Perhaps there was a psychological connection between his embracing religion just as his oil business was collapsing. He addressed the connection when he wrote: "I believe my spiritual awakening started well before the price of oil went below $9 [a barrel]." But he also admitted: "[But 1986 was] a year of change when I look back at it. I really never have connected the dots all the way."

One source of inspiration for the Bush family had always been the Baptist minister, Billy Graham. Graham was an old friend of the family. He and his wife, Ruth, had visited the Bushes at their home in Kennebunkport, Maine, every summer for several years, and Graham had preached at two churches the Bush family attended. On those weekends, the family would invite Graham to their home and talk with him. During the summer of 1985, George W. spoke with Graham alone. Bush would later write about it in his book, *A Charge to Keep*:

> Over the course of that weekend, Reverend Graham planted a mustard seed in my soul, a seed that grew over the next year. He led me to the path, and I began walking. And it was the beginning of a change in my life. I had always been a religious person, had regularly attended church, even taught Sunday school and served as an altar boy. But that weekend my faith took on new meaning. It was the beginning of a new walk where I would re-commit my heart to Jesus Christ. I was humbled to learn that God sent His Son to die for a sinner like me.

George W. spent that fall as a member of an all-male

Bible study group. Approximately 120 men gathered and discussed scriptures and how their lives were being changed. To George, "the words [of the Bible] became clearer and more meaningful."

While George W.'s religious change brought spiritual redirection to his life, he had more difficulty with another long-term problem—drinking. By the mid-1980s, he had been arrested while drunk on more than one occasion, once after stealing a Christmas wreath off someone's door. He had also been arrested for drunk driving. By the time he had reached age forty, it was clear that his drinking was a problem. Several times he spent more than one day drinking. When a friend asked him if he could remember a day when he had not had a beer, George W. admitted he could not. Then, in July 1986, while George W. and Laura were staying at the Broadmoor Hotel in Colorado Springs celebrating their anniversary with friends, he woke one morning with a terrible hangover. He tried to take his morning jog, but had to stop halfway. He was feeling his age and the physical toll that his lifestyle was taking. He returned to his hotel room and told Laura that he was going to stop drinking. Today, Bush credits both Laura's support and Billy Graham's inspiration with helping him to quit drinking.

The next two years after he stopped drinking were critical ones for his family. As the last term of the Reagan presidency wound down, George W.'s father was planning another run for president. This time he was the

The entire Bush family gathers at their family home in Maine in the 1980s.
(Courtesy of the George Bush Presidential Library.)

heavily favored front runner. A newly focused and sober George W., who had little to keep him busy in his job at Harken Oil, was eager to help get his father elected.

In the spring of 1987, George and Laura packed up the twins, then five years old, and moved to Washington, D.C. They lived in a townhouse just a mile away from his parents. The move was difficult. They had grown fond of their lives in Midland, where they had bought a house and remodeled it to their liking. But family duty and politics called them east.

Much was at stake in the election. Everyone working on the Bush campaign understood that, should the vice president lose the election, it would probably signal the end of his political career. George W. saw his role as a loyalty enforcer. He dogged the campaign workers, even the highly-paid political advisors, such as Lee Atwater, who was the main force in the campaign.

One aspect of campaigning George W. did not like was the constant media presence. He often found himself fielding an endless barrage of questions and rumors. When a story began to circulate that his father had been carrying on a long-term sexual affair with his secretary, Jennifer Fitzgerald, it was George W. who argued that the stories were not true. Moving to Washington and working closely with his father brought them closer together than they had been in years. Once again they had Sunday afternoon hamburger cookouts, and Barbara had time to spend with her granddaughters.

After a relentless campaign against Democrat Michael Dukakis, the Governor of Massachusetts, George Herbert Walker Bush won the presidential election in November 1988. Now the prestigious Bush family had produced a president. The campaign also renewed George W.'s taste for politics. At age forty-two, however, he still felt uncertain about his own future, both in and out of politics. He was still living in his father's shadow. He seriously considered running for governor of Texas and bought a home in Dallas and quietly let it be known he was open to a candidacy. But friends and family convinced him he

President George Bush and First Lady Barbara Bush are pictured in front of the White House with former President of Russia Boris Yeltsin. *(Courtesy of the Library of Congress.)*

needed more statewide exposure first. Also, there was the question of money—George did not have enough to finance a gubernatorial campaign. Then an opportunity fell into his lap that made him set aside his political ambitions.

George W. was asked to join a group of businessmen who planned to buy the Texas Rangers baseball team. The owner, Eddie Chiles, wanted to sell, and Bush was asked to find investors. He sold some of his stock in Harken Oil, netted $500,000 and threw part of the money into the pool with the others he convinced to join the venture. Bush and a colleague were asked to serve as the team's operators. He would receive a salary of $200,000 to serve as the public relations coordinator for the Rangers.

The change from the oil business to the popular world of baseball proved to be a great move for George W. Sports ran in the Bush family blood. His great uncle Herbert Walker had been an original investor in the New York Mets; his father had excelled in sports at Yale; and George had grown up memorizing baseball statistics and dreaming of playing in the major league. He had found a comfortable niche for himself—one which would gain him statewide attention and popularity.

When George W. joined the Texas Rangers management team, the Rangers were a losing team. Games were poorly attended, and the stadium was out-of-date and rundown. George set out immediately to change the image of the Rangers. He created a network of supporters, put the club on friendly terms with the media, and helped to develop pitcher Nolan Ryan's image as the team's super player. He increased regional interest in the Rangers' games by arranging for Spanish radio broadcasts to appeal to the Hispanic community. Bush's management style was friendly and personable. He worked hard to know each club employee—from groundskeeper to the food vendors—by name and was almost always present at games. He loved walking around the park, hailing employees, and shaking hands. His designated seat—section 109, row 1, seat 8—was near the team's dugout, where he could talk to players, enjoy the game, eat hot dogs and peanuts, and sign autographs. Other than Nolan Ryan, George W. Bush was the public face of the Texas Rangers. His efforts began to pay off as both he and the club became more popular.

Laura and the twins also attended the games. George W. wrote in his autobiography:

> For five years, Laura and I went to fifty or sixty home games a year. I always say if you're going to a baseball game, you had better go with someone you like, because you have ample time to talk. I went with someone I loved. And talk we did: about baseball, about our girls, about life. It was a time of family and friends.

During his years with the franchise, Bush campaigned heavily, not on behalf of a politician running for office, but for a new stadium for the Rangers. Just after he joined the club, a plan was under development for a new ballpark. The effort to convince the public to help finance the park put Bush in the public eye as a political figure, as well as a spokesman for an investment group. In the end, through his efforts, Texan voters agreed on a tax increase that generated over $100 million for the stadium. It was Bush's biggest achievement during his years with the Rangers.

The new park, simply called the Ballpark in Arlington, opened in April 1994. The stadium was full, concert pianist Van Cliburn played "The Star Spangled Banner," and the mayor of Arlington threw out the first pitch. The park included a restaurant, museum, and sports bar.

Finally, George W. had earned some success in a venture unlike any his father had attempted. But the success also brought controversy. In the summer of 1990, he sold off his remaining shares of Harken stock to pay off his part of the debt created when his team of investors had purchased the Texas Rangers franchise. When the Persian Gulf War broke out less than two months later, the price of Harken stock crashed. George was accused of having inside knowledge about the looming crisis in the Middle East. He insisted he had just sold the stock when he needed the cash. He was also questioned when Harken Energy Corporation received significant oil drill-

When George W. joined the management team of the Texas Rangers, he strived to make Texas baseball popular and entertaining. This success gave him the opportunity to step out of his father's shadow and also to build a strong and positive relationship with the public.

(Courtesy of the George Bush Presidential Library.)

ing rights in the Persian Gulf. Some thought that he had used his influence to get Harken the contracts. Few oil companies the size of Harken's had ever received such privileges. Again, George W. denied the charges.

After Iraqi leader Saddam Hussein led the invasion of the Middle Eastern nation of Kuwait, President Bush rallied the western powers and various Middle Eastern nations to join with him in a war against Iraq. The war lasted only a matter of weeks in the spring of 1991, ending with American and allied victory. President Bush's popularity soared, but it did not last long.

After the victory in Kuwait, President Bush could have turned his attention to domestic affairs. The country had been in a recession through most of 1991, and many people wanted the government to do more to revive the economy. But the administration argued that it was a natural business cycle that would soon end. This turned out to be a political mistake.

The 1992 Bush reelection campaign was also hampered because Lee Atwater, whose loyalty had been questioned by George W. during his father's election, was dying of a brain tumor. Atwater's "take no prisoners" style of politics had devastated Michael Dukakis in 1988. George W. was busy with his work with the Texas ball club and had little time to devote to the campaign. On April 25, George W. took a symbolic chunk out of the old Arlington Stadium parking lot with a front-end loader as the construction got underway.

After a tough reelection campaign, George Bush lost the presidency to Democrat Bill Clinton and his running mate, Al Gore, in 1992. *(Courtesy of the Library of Congress.)*

After facing stiff primary competition, President Bush entered the fall campaign running against Democratic nominee Bill Clinton and his running mate Tennessee Senator Al Gore. In addition, another Texan, billionaire H. Ross Perot, had entered the race as a third party candidate. Bush's poll numbers dropped throughout the summer. After the Persian Gulf War the previous year, Bush's approval rating had stood at an impressive eighty-nine percent. By early August of 1992, his approval polls dropped to a miserable twenty-nine percent. People repeatedly told pollsters that they did not think that Bush cared enough about the middle class. In November, Bill

Clinton defeated President Bush. (The previous month, another Bush political defeat had occurred. The twins, now nearly eleven years old, both ran for Student Council offices at their school and lost.)

The presidential defeat hurt the entire family. Victory had seemed assured less than a year ago, and now President Bush was forced out of office by a relatively unknown governor of neighboring Arkansas. The defeat marked the end of George Bush's political career. He had served as congressman, ambassador, CIA director, Republican Party chair, vice president, and Chief Executive. Now it was time for George W. to make a run for an office his father had never held—governor of Texas.

Chapter Seven

Abandoning the Sidelines

On November 8, 1993, George W. traveled to four major Texas cities—Austin, Dallas, Houston, and San Antonio—to announce his intention to run for the office of governor of Texas. He told the state's voters that he wanted to "abandon the sidelines and get in the middle of trying to improve my state." He sold his interest in the Texas Rangers the following spring. He made $15 million off the sale of the franchise but, as he later wrote, "The sale was bittersweet . . . because I have so many wonderful memories of my time in baseball."

As the campaign started, his opponents charged that George W. was cashing in on his family name. It also did not take long before incidents from his partying days became public knowledge.

The incumbent opponent, Governor Ann Richards, was well-liked by the people of Texas. She was a favorite of the state and national press, a tough-talking, shoot-

from-the-hip, motorcycle-riding politician. Some of
George W.'s friends had suggested he postpone his race
another four years. One told him: "You've got a popular
incumbent Democrat that you can't beat. It would be
suicide." His professional and family life was happy.
Laura stayed busy with charity work, the girls enjoyed
school, and they lived in a very comfortable North Dallas home. But George W. would not be deterred. His
brother, Jeb Bush, who had moved to Florida years
before, also decided to run for governor of his adopted
home state.

During the campaign, George W. hammered at what
he perceived to be Richards's weak spots. Richards wanted
to see property tax monies from rich neighborhoods
shifted to pay for poorer schools outside of their home
districts. George W. opposed the plan because he thought
voters in the wealthy school districts would too. He also
wanted to cap the amount of money that could be awarded
in liability lawsuits. One of his more controversial positions was to reform the state's welfare system. George W.
suggested that welfare recipients not receive benefits for
any more than two children. He also suggested that part
of the social safety net be provided by private charities
and businesses.

The campaign fight between George W. Bush and
Ann Richards was loud, boisterous, and sometimes ugly.
Governor Richards attempted to convince Texans that
Bush, who had been raised in Midland and returned

there after his education, was an elite outsider. She referred to George W. Bush as "Shrub," implying he was less than his father and was only riding on his coattails.

One of the most difficult accusations for George W. to explain away was the indiscretion of his youth: the drinking, poor grades in school, and alleged drug use. There were stories of the younger Bush having danced naked in a bar while under the influence of alcohol, or, perhaps, cocaine. When Bush refused to emphatically state he had never used illegal drugs—"Maybe I did, maybe I didn't. What's the relevance?"—it led to more questions from reporters.

George W. refused to meet Governor Richards's accusations with taunts of his own. He attempted to remain focused on the issues. Eventually, Richards went too far. While addressing a teachers' group in Texarkana, she said: "You just work like a dog, you do well, and all of a sudden you've got some jerk who's running for public office telling everybody it's all a sham." The reaction to the "jerk" comment was overwhelmingly negative. The amount of money George was able to raise also helped him. Richards was also hurt because 1994 turned out to be a strong Republican year, with the GOP taking control of both houses of the federal Congress for the first time since the 1950s. On election day, 1994, George W. Bush was elected by a sizable margin.

Because Texas was the second largest state in the Union, Bush's victory was significant nationally. It was also important to the family, because Richards had been a fierce opponent of his father when he was president. Although Jeb lost his race in Florida, a happy Bush family was present at George W.'s swearing-in as governor of Texas. The Reverend Billy Graham delivered the invocation. After assuming office, he enlarged his gubernatorial office space and decorated it with a mahogany desk his father had passed on to him, family photos, and his collection of 250 autographed baseballs.

As governor, George W. Bush's daily routine included three office hours in the morning, a mid-day jog, followed by an afternoon of meetings and visitors. Many evenings, he and Laura played host in the governor's mansion to an official state dinner. Each day might vary in its details, but the governor was always firm about one thing: by 9 p.m., his official day was over, providing him with some family time with Laura and the girls.

He worked to keep the avenues of communication open. He listened to his advisors and staff members, although they were instructed to keep their rhetoric to a minimum and to quickly get to their point. George W. was a good listener and absorbed information well. He had come a long way since his college days.

One criticism leveled against Governor Bush was his tendency to spend too much time and attention on his "pet projects." Subjects such as minority appointments to state government jobs and protecting the environment took a back seat during Bush's first term. He had promised during the campaign to improve education in Texas. He attempted early in his administration to change the way public schools receive funding. He did not favor a system based on personal property taxation, because it often provided better-funded schools in wealthier neighborhoods. Instead, he supported a raise in the state sales tax to pay for education improvements. But this plan received heavy opposition and was roundly defeated. It was most unpopular within his own party, which was opposed to raising taxes. He was eventually able to push through increases in school funding.

Bush also worked to raise school test scores. One of his programs to raise scores was the Texas Reading Initiative. The program was designed to help each student in public school reach reading proficiency by the third grade. After implementation of the program, student test scores made significant improvements. Math scores also rose, and scores in all other subjects had improved.

Another political goal for Governor Bush was to restructure the state's juvenile justice system. Under Bush, juveniles in prison were no longer allowed to wear gang colors. They were expected to work while in prison and to remain silent with guards unless they were spoken to first. Youthful offenders had their heads shaved.

In addition to such political changes, the Bush administration worked to reduce welfare programs across the state, and to encourage corporations to move to Texas.

All these issues—education, juvenile crime, welfare and corporate investment in Texas—had been key campaign issues. With a clear focus, George W. worked to bring about change in these areas. He continued to work on his agenda despite the fact that Democrats held a majority of the seats in the Texas state house. Early in his administration, he met with nearly all the state senators in an effort to gain their support.

As Texas's First Lady, Laura Bush became involved in her favorite projects. As a former schoolteacher and librarian, she supported early childhood development programs to encourage parents to prepare their children for school. In 1996, she helped to organize the Texas Book Festival, which focuses on books by Texas authors. The annual festival helps raise money to support Texas public libraries.

George W.'s reelection in 1998 was never in question. Democrat Garry Mauro, the state's Land Commissioner, opposed him. Mauro was hurt when one hundred of the state's leading Democratic politicians endorsed George W. Among them was Bob Bullock, the Democratic lieutenant governor, one of the most powerful party men in Texas. Bullock's move was extraordinary considering his longstanding Democratic politics and the fact that he was Mauro's daughter's godfather.

In November 1998, George W. won sixty-seven percent of the vote. One out of every four Democratic voters cast ballots for him. He received fifty percent of the

Former president George Bush was proud to see his first son serve as governor of Texas.
(Courtesy of the George Bush Presidential Library.)

Hispanic vote and twenty-seven percent of the African-American vote, unprecedented for a Republican politician. Two out of every three women voters supported George, as did three out of every four independents.

No sooner had the reelection campaign ended than the possibility of a new campaign loomed ahead for George W. Bush. After such an impressive victory in Texas, the pressure began to build for George W. to make a run for the U.S. presidency in the year 2000. He began to seriously consider the possibility when a national poll indicated that Republican voters would support him over all other likely contenders. In his autobiography, Bush wrote about hearing of the poll for the first time:

> It all started in the summer of 1997, when Karen Hughes walked into my office with a smile on her face and a scrap of paper in her hand. 'You're leading in the poll,' she said. 'What poll?' I asked. 'The poll that shows you are the front-runner for the Republican presidential nomination,' she replied. At the time it seemed surreal, but the speculation soon began to mount. By the fall of 1997, I couldn't get on an elevator or walk through the back of a hotel kitchen on the way to make a speech without someone saying, 'Governor, please run for President.'

For Bush and others, the possibility of a presidential

race against Democratic candidate Vice President Al Gore carried an added emotional weight. It was the Clinton-Gore ticket that had defeated his father's bid for reelection in 1992. The prospect of Bush's son defeating Gore eight years later would be a sweet revenge for many Republicans, including most of the Bush family.

Bush told the media he would make his intentions known concerning a presidential bid following the 1998 gubernatorial race. Until the day of his inauguration for a second term, Bush claimed to be undecided on whether to run. During the inaugural ceremonies, a minister spoke to the assembled crowd, emphasizing the need in America for leaders who exemplify good moral values and honest government. Bush later wrote: "Pastor Mark Craig had prodded me out of my comfortable life as Governor of Texas and toward a national campaign."

As Bush prepared to embark on his presidential quest, he understood the challenges ahead. Al Gore was a seasoned campaigner and the son of a political family. His father had served in the Senate.

Once Bush had decided to run for president, he began formulating an agenda. He attempted to establish his image as a "compassionate conservative," holding on to traditional conservative views, such as supporting a strong national defense policy, a balanced budget, tax cuts, smaller government, and fewer social programs. But, by portraying himself as a compassionate version of a Republican conservative, Bush was able to appeal to more moderate voters as well. The difference was sometimes subtle to the point of being indistinguishable, but the rhetoric was effective.

He still supported school vouchers, for example. Education reform was a serious issue in the 2000 election. Republicans favored school vouchers, state certified credits which could be used by parents to remove their children from public school and place them in a private school. Democrats charged that simply moving students to private schools did not address the larger issue of improving public schools. Debates raged over this issue throughout the election, but George W. felt it was necessary to maintain his position to gain the support of the conservative majority in the Republican Party. He justified his position as the best way to "not trap students in low-performing schools." The "compassionate conservative" label worked as an effective electoral strategy.

There were other factors that worked to George W.'s advantage. He had a recognizable political name, he was a successful Texas governor who had displayed skill in winning votes outside of his core constituency, and he appealed to the Christian Right with his story of religious conversion. Also, George W.'s personable style connected with the voters. The same pleasing personality that had carried him through much of his life, from Andover to the oil business to Texas politics, helped him to work the crowds on a national level. One reporter assessed George W.'s style with the following observations: "I never once saw his eyes stray from a voter to survey the room. Bush is a toucher: He doesn't shake your hand so much as grab it: he leans in close, clutches an arm, pats a shoulder, gives a hug. 'Hey, buddy,' he'll say, or 'Preciate you takin' the time.' "

Throughout the campaign Bush was criticized for his environmental record. Smog levels in Texas' largest metropolitan communities had risen during his tenure as governor. Texas grew to have one of the worst air quality ratings in the nation. He was also attacked for his veto of a plan to reduce the authority and power of the state's managed-care health organizations, which many people thought put profits in front of patients' health care. Given his mediocre academic record and tendency to speak simply with a Texan drawl, many charged that George W. was incompetent. This last point made him a favorite topic of late night comedy skits. However, despite these negative criticisms, Bush maintained a significant lead in the pre-primary stage of the campaign.

Then the Bush campaign was shocked by a loss in the first primary in New Hampshire to Republican challenger, Senator John McCain of Arizona. But George W.'s momentum returned when he won the South Carolina primary. Then McCain won the Michigan primary on February 22, much to Bush's surprise. Following the Michigan vote, Bush began emphasizing the differences between McCain and himself. He claimed that he was a Washington outsider, while McCain was part of the

"Beltway" problem, implying that Washington politicians were corrupt and dishonest. During the first week of March, Bush won victories in California and New York, as well as Georgia, Maryland, Maine, and Missouri. These losses effectively ended McCain's campaign.

At the end of the primaries, George W. Bush and Al Gore were running even in the polls. Political experts were predicting a close election. By the end of July 2000, an ABC News/Washington Post poll pegged Bush slightly ahead of Gore.

Later that summer, as the two candidates prepared for their party conventions, they announced their picks for vice presidential running mates. Vice President Gore selected Joseph Lieberman, a Senator from Connecticut. Lieberman was the first Jewish nominee for nation-wide office. Bush chose Richard "Dick" Cheney, who had served as the Secretary of Defense under his father.

Throughout his campaign, George W. actively sought the votes of minorities. He met with the leaders of the NAACP, and his campaign worked hard to distance itself from old line Republican rhetoric, such as the anti-immigrant positions many party members had taken throughout the 1990s. Despite Bush's work courting minority votes, the two candidates remained even in the polls. Bush's determination to win never flagged. During a mid-September CNN interview, Bush said, "My supporters have got to know something: They're working hard and I'm working hard right along with them."

During the month before the November 7 election, Bush and Gore participated in a series of televised debates. While the controlled forums brought the two candidates face-to-face, giving each an opportunity to present his case directly to the voters, the debates did not result in any significant change in support. Both the vice president and the Texas governor performed reasonably well. In fact, by the second debate, the two candidates found themselves frequently agreeing with one another. As one CNN reporter put it, "Each man seemed to go out of his way to say, 'We don't disagree on this issue.' "

Then, just three days before the election, a news story broke out reporting that Governor Bush had been convicted of drunk driving in 1976, even though he had claimed two years earlier he had not been arrested at any time after 1968. Bush fended off the accusation, charging that Gore and the Democrats released the information as a "dirty trick."

The accusation against Bush appeared to come after most people had decided whom they would vote for. The weekend before the election, George W. was campaigning in Florida, a state he knew he must win to defeat Gore. That day, Reverend Billy Graham endorsed Bush for president.

On November 7, 2000, candidates Bush and Gore became part of the closest, most complicated—and certainly the longest—election in U.S. history. It began on election night and continued for the following five weeks.

George W. and his opponent, Al Gore, participated in three televised debates.
(AP Photo/EdReinke.)

Election night began with a series of errors on the part of the major television networks. As the results came back placing the contenders neck and neck, Florida, with its twenty-five electoral votes, became the state that would push one candidate into the winner's circle. First Al Gore was declared the winner of the electoral votes of Florida—making an electoral victory by Bush unlikely. If he could not win Florida, the very state where his gubernatorial brother, Jeb, (who after a second attempt, was elected the governor of Florida in 1998) had campaigned heavily for him, how could he be expected to win?

As the night progressed, however, the voter count in Florida became less of a sure thing for Gore. By 2 a.m. (EST), the networks determined they had erred in calling Florida for Gore. They then announced Bush as the winner of Florida. Gore telephoned the Texas governor to congratulate him on his win and to concede the election. But just as Gore was about to make his concession speech, the networks changed their projections again and called Florida "too close to call." Gore called Bush and retracted his concession. Although many Americans went to bed in the wee hours of the post-election morning believing Bush had won the election, the next morning they woke to a new reality: Neither candidate had received enough electoral votes (a minimum of 270 votes was needed) to be declared president. Most importantly, Florida was still too close to call.

The nation's attention turned to Florida, where a recount of the votes was ordered. Controversy soon focused on how ballots were being counted in various Florida precincts and polling stations. Voter confusion and inconsistencies in ballot counting (along with a sizable number of absentee ballots from overseas voters) became the focal point of the heated post-election controversy. More than 19,000 votes were disqualified in West Palm Beach, Florida, due to problems from the confusing design of the "butterfly" ballot. Voters in that heavily Democratic county claimed to have accidentally voted for Reform Party candidate Pat Buchanan instead of Al Gore. In addition, several thousand ballots were mechanically rejected when voting machines could not detect punched votes on ballot cards, raising questions as to the reliability of machines.

Court cases were filed on both sides. For the next several weeks, the fate of the election hung in the balance. As the state deadline for the vote's final report loomed, voting officials in three Florida counties painstakingly worked through a hand count of the ballots. The outcome of the hand count appeared to hinge on the ability of officials to interpret whether a voter intended to vote for a particular candidate based on the partial removal of the ballot's "chads," small rectangular pieces designed to be punched through and removed when a voter made his or her choice. The question was whether to count the chads that had not been completely punched out. In the midst of all the confusion, charges, and counter-charges from both campaigns, Bush's running mate, Dick Cheney, suffered a heart attack.

The Florida Supreme Court ordered a manual recount of all ballots. The Bush lawyers appealed this decision to the United States Supreme Court, which overturned the Florida Supreme Court's decision on December 13. The U.S. Supreme Court vote was close, 5-4, and immediately controversial. The decision was further clouded because seven of the justices agreed that hand counting violated constitutional guarantees of equal protection and due process because no uniform standard for deter-

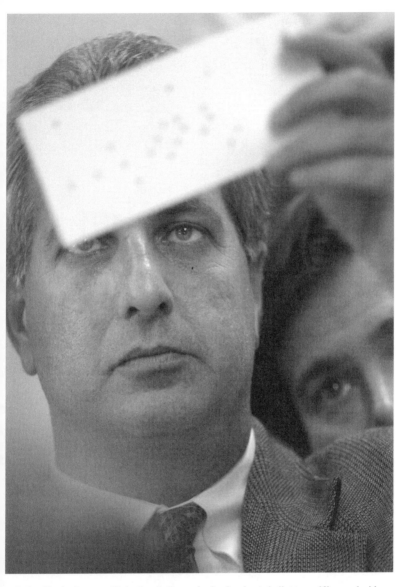

Judge Charles Burton of Palm Beach County looks closely at a ballot to see if he can decide which candidate the voter intended to choose. Due to confusing ballots in parts of Florida, officials demanded a manual recount in certain counties. *(AP Photo/LM Otero, File)*

mining a voter's intent was in place. Earlier, Florida Secretary of State, Katherine Harris, a Republican, had certified the election and granted Florida's twenty-five electoral votes for Bush. Now that certification had been upheld.

On December 14, Vice President Al Gore went on national television and conceded the election. The final, official electoral vote was Bush 271, Gore 266. But the popular election results told a different story: Gore, 50,996,116—Bush, 50,456,169. Gore earned almost a half million more votes than the new president. Some angry Democrats refused to agree that Bush was elected, preferring instead to uphold that he had been *selected* by the U.S. Supreme Court. The first presidential election of the new century had proven to be one of the closest and most controversial elections in American history.

Bush spoke to the American people for the first time as undisputed president-elect on December 13. He said that he understood the divisions that existed between Americans following the highly divisive electoral process. "I was not elected to serve one party, but to serve one nation," Bush said in his address.

During the five weeks of delay between the November election and the Supreme Court decision, Bush organized his new administration. His running mate, Dick Cheney, headed the Bush transition team. As Bush selected those who would serve in his cabinet and in other significant positions, he sometimes looked back to his

George W. chose Richard "Dick" Cheney as his vice presidential running mate. During the ballot controversy in Florida, Cheney suffered a heart attack. *(AP Photo/Ron Edmonds.)*

father's administration. Cheney, of course, had been secretary of defense. Andrew Card, who had served as secretary of transportation in the first Bush administration, was chosen to be White House chief of staff. New Secretary of State Colin Powell had previously served as army chief of staff.

The night before the inauguration, George W. Bush attended ten balls. He danced with Laura, although he joked that he lacked skill as a dancer. The next morning, January 20, was a Saturday. George W., Laura, and the twins, Jenna and Barbara, stood together on the Capitol steps under a gray, rainy sky. George W.'s father stood next to his son and watched him take the oath of office. George swore his oath with his hand on an old family Bible, the same one used by his father when he had taken the presidential oath back in 1989. After being sworn in as the nation's 43rd president, George W. Bush spoke for only fifteen minutes. He called for the nation to embrace an era of "civility, courage, compassion, and character."

As the Bush administration began, the new president had the opportunity to govern with Republican control of both houses of Congress. He began working to push through his campaign agenda of education reform and tax cuts. Congress soon approved a tax bill, calling for cuts equal to $1.35 trillion stretched out over ten years. He worked with Massachusetts Senator Edward Kennedy to raise the amount of federal money spent on public education. George W., when asked of his assessment of his first three months in office, said his first season had been "pretty darn good." He added: "I am enthusiastic about the job. I really love what I am doing."

This positive attitude suffered a setback in May 2001, however, when Republican Senator Jim Jeffords of Vermont decided to leave the party. This threw control of the evenly divided Senate to the Democrats. After making his decision, Jeffords said he felt uncomfortable with the direction of the Bush administration. He disagreed with Bush's efforts to open more public lands to oil and gas drilling, and to a presidential order that increased the amount of arsenic allowed in drinking water. Mining companies had asked Bush to raise the levels because arsenic was used in their operations. Jeffords also said he thought the Republican Party had grown too conservative under Bush.

By late spring of 2001, the Florida State Senate overwhelmingly approved an election reform package, designed to eliminate punchcard ballots, hoping to prevent any possible future repeat of their election nightmare.

Due to the close race in 2000, President George W. Bush faced a difficult challenge uniting an almost equally divided Congress and nation. He stated in his first presidential address to the country: "The president of the United States is the president of every single American, of every race and every background. Whether you voted for me or not, I will do my best to serve your interests, and I will work to earn your respect." Although time alone will show how successfully the first president of the new century will govern, George W. Bush is truly a man who has successfully combined the dreams of his forefathers with his own aspirations.

Timeline

1945—George Herbert Walker Bush marries Barbara Pierce in Rye, New York, on January 6.

1946—George Walker Bush is born in New Haven, Connecticut, on July 6.

1948—The Bush family moves to Odessa, Texas, in June.

1949—Sister Pauline Robinson Bush (Robin) is born on December 20.

1953—Brother John Ellis Bush (Jeb) is born on February 11.

—Robin dies of leukemia on October 12.

1955—Brother Neil Mallon Bush is born on January 22.

1956—Brother Marvin Pierce Bush is born on October 22.

1959—Family moves to Houston, Texas, in August.

—Sister Dorothy Ellis Bush (Doro) is born on August 18.

1961—Fifteen-year-old George W. leaves Texas to attend Phillips Academy at Andover, Massachusetts, in the fall.

1964—Graduates from Andover; is accepted to Yale University.

1967—Announces engagement to Cathryn Wolfman in January; wedding never takes place.

1968—Joins the Skull & Bones; graduates from Yale.
—Joins the Texas Air National Guard.

1969—Trains for National Guard throughout the entire year.

1970—Begins service in Texas Air National Guard.

1973—Works as volunteer for Professionals United for Leadership League (Project PULL) and works with inner city kids during the summer.
—Begins attending Harvard School of Business.

1975—Graduates from Harvard School of Business.
—Returns to Midland, Texas, and works in the oil business until 1980.

1977—Meets and courts school librarian, Laura Welch.
—Marries Laura Welch at the United Methodist Church in Midland, Texas, on November 6.

1978—Runs and loses election of the Texas 19th Congressional Seat race

1981—Laura and George W. become parents of twins, Jenna and Barbara, on November 28.

1985—Recommits his life to his Christian faith.

1986—Decides to quit drinking.

1987—George W., Laura, and the twins move to Washington, D.C., to help in his father's bid for election to the U.S. presidency.

1988—Becomes involved in deal to purchase the Texas Rangers baseball franchise.

1989—Serves as public relations director for the Texas Rangers until 1994.

1993—Announces in November his intentions to run for the governorship of Texas.

1994—Elected as Texas governor, winning over incumbent, Ann Richards.

1994—Serves as Texas governor, including two years of a second four-year term, until 2000.

1998—Reelected as Texas governor.

2000—Actively campaigns as Republican candidate for the U.S. presidency.

—Election results on November 7 do not produce a clear winner in the presidential race between George W. Bush and Vice President Al Gore.

—U.S. Supreme Court Justices determine, by a vote of five to four, on December 12 that all vote recounts in Florida must end.

—Vice President Al Gore delivers his concession speech on national television on December 14.

2001—George W. Bush takes the oath of office on January 20, becoming the 43rd president.

Sources

Chapter One: East Meets West

p. 22, "I bet she can see . . ." Bill Minutaglio, *First Son: George W. Bush and the Bush Family Dynasty* (New York: Random House, 1999), 45.

Chapter Two: "The Lip"

p. 26, "This was a period . . ." Elizabeth Mitchell, *W: Revenge of the Bush Dynasty* (New York: Hyperion, 2000), 45.

p. 29, "I'm sure he took some . . ." Ibid., 66.

p. 29, "Take one good look . . ." Mitchell, *Revenge,* 45.

Chapter Three: The "Nomadic Period"

p. 34, "I knew your father . . ." Romano and Lardner Jr, "Following His Father's Path, Step by Step by Step," *Washington Post*, July 27, 1999.

p. 36, "the sternest words . . ." Doug Wead, *Man of Integrity* (Eugene, Oregon: Harvest House, 1988), 118.

p. 38, "there was something . . ." Minutaglio, *First Son,* 99.

p. 38, "I loved him . . ." J. H. Hatfield, *Fortunate Son: George W. Bush and the Making of an American President* (New York City: Soft Skull Press, 2000), 37.

Chapter Four: Emerging from the Shadow

p. 44, "He was certainly competent . . ." Minutaglio, *First Son,* 126.

p. 45, "George W. clearly stands out . . ." Mitchell, *Revenge,* 131.

p. 48, "I hear you're looking . . ." Ibid, 139.

p. 48, "[I was trying to] reconcile . . ." Ibid, 139.

p. 49, "[He] was so down to earth . . ." Ibid, 139.

p. 49, "He would love to see . . ." Mitchell, *Revenge,* 140.

p. 55, "If it wasn't love . . ." George W. Bush, *A Charge to Keep: My Journey to the White House*, New York: HarperCollins, 1999), 79.

p. 55, "struck by lightning . . ." Mitchell, *Revenge,* 161.

Chapter Five: A Life of His Own

p. 56, "I think the timing . . ." Ibid, 161.

p. 57, "Well, your speech . . ." Minutaglio, *First Son*, 186.

p. 60, "Laura and I didn't know . . ." Bush, *A Charge,* 85.

p. 61, "a friend once told me . . ." Ibid, 86.

Chapter Six: A Clearer, More Meaningful Life

p. 64, "I believe my spiritual awakening . . ." Mitchell, *Revenge,* 198.

p. 65, "Over the course of . . ." Bush, *A Charge*, 136.

p. 66, "the words of the Bible . . ." Ibid, 137.

p. 71, "For five years . . ." Bush, *A Charge*, 206.

Chapter Seven: Abandoning the Sidelines

p. 77, "abandon the sidelines . . ." Mitchell, *Revenge*, 297.

p. 77, "The sale was bittersweet . . ." Bush, *A Charge*, 206.

p. 78, "You've got a popular incumbent . . ." Mitchell, *A Charge*, 294.

p. 79, "Maybe I did . . ." Minutaglio, *First Son*, 281.

p. 79, "You just work like a dog . . ." Mitchell, *Revenge*, 307.

p. 84, "It all started . . ." Bush, *A Charge*, 222-223.

p. 85, "Pastor Mark Craig . . ." Ibid., 13.

p. 86, "I never once saw . . ." Paul Burka, "The W. Nobody Knows: What He's Like in Real Life," *Texas Monthly*, June 1999, 7.

p. 88, "My supporters have got to . . ." CNN's "Evans, Novak, Hunt and Shields," September 17, 2000.

p. 89, "Each man seemed to go out . . ." Quote from CNN reporter, William Schneider, taken from website: www.geocities.com/CapitolHill/6228/pres2000/bush.html.

p. 94, "I was not elected . . ." George W. Bush speech, December 13, 2000, Texas House of Representatives.

p. 97, "I am enthusiastic . . ." John King, CNN Washington Bureau, " 'Pretty darn good,' Bush calls his first 100 days," CNN website, April 25, 2001: www.cnn.com/2001/ALLPOLITICS/04/25/bush.interview/

p. 97, "The president of the United States . . ." George W. Bush speech, December 13, 2000.

Bibliography

Bush, Barbara. *Barbara Bush: A Memoir*. New York: St.
Martin's Press, 1994.

Bush, George. *All the Best, George Bush: My Life in
Letters and Other Writings*. New York: Scribner,
1999.

Bush, George W. *A Charge to Keep: My Journey to the
White House*. New York: HarperCollins, 2001. (A
Perennial Imprint).

Dionne, E.J. and William Kristol. *Bush V. Gore: The
Court Cases and the Commentary*. Washington,
D.C.: Brookings Institution Press, 2001.

Gormley, Beatrice. *President George W. Bush: Our
Forty-third President*. New York: Simon & Schuster
Children's, 2001.

Hatfield, J. H. H. *Fortunate Son: George W. Bush and
the Making of an American President*. New York
City: Soft Skull Press, Inc., 1999.

Ivins, Molly. *Shrub: The Short but Happy Political Life
of George W. Bush*. New York: Random House,
Incorporated, 2000.

McNeese, Tim. *The U.S. Presidency*. St. Louis: Milliken Publishing Company, 2001.

Minutaglio, Bill. *First Son: George W. Bush and the Bush Family Dynasty*. New York: Times Books, Random House, 1999.

Mitchell, Elizabeth. *W: Revenge of the Bush Dynasty*. New York: Hyperion, 2000.

Olasky, Marvin. *Compassionate Conservatism: What It Is, What It Does, and How It Can Transform America*. New York: The Free Press, Simon & Schuster, 2000.

Romano, Lois and George Lardner, Jr. "Bush's Life-Changing Year," *Washington Post*, July 25, 1999.

———. "Tragedy Created Bush Mother-Son Bond," *Washington Post*, July 26, 1999.

———. "So-So Student but a Campus Mover," *Washington Post*, July 27, 1999.

———. "At Height of Vietnam, Bush Picks Guard," *Washington Post*, July 28, 1999.

———. "Young Bush, a Political Natural, Revs Up," *Washington Post*, July 29, 1999.

———. "Bush Name Helps Fuel Oil Dealings," *Washington Post*, July 30, 1999.

———. "Bush's Move Up to the Majors," *Washington Post*, July 31, 1999.

Wukovits, John F. *George W. Bush*. San Diego: Lucent Books, 2000.

Websites

Bush-Cheney 2000, Inc.
www.georgewbush.com

George Bush Presidential Library and Museum
http://bushlibrary.tamu.edu

The White House, Washington, D.C.
www.whitehouse.gov

Index